Running Wild with Bossy Boy

Hui Zhou

※※※ Hui Zhou•Nova Scotia•Canada ※※※

Text and Photograph Copyright © 2018 Hui Zhou

ISBN 978-1-77513-980-5

Design: Hui Zhou
Editor/Guide: Diane Tibert

Printed at Halcraft Printers Inc., Halifax, Nova Scotia, Canada

Hui Zhou
Nova Scotia, Canada 2018

Foreword

Chickens are one of the most common and widely spread domestic animals in human history.

To Hui, raising her own chickens was a long held dream. It came from childhood helping her grandparents feed chickens running freely in their family's yard in Beijing, China.

Because of population growth and city development, concrete apartment buildings replaced most yards and houses. Those free-running chickens soon became memories hidden away in her dreams.

Today, most chickens world-wide are raised in commercial settings either as egg layers in body-sized cages or as meat birds over-weighted in only a couple of months. This is a twisted life. It ends up with a huge loss to chickens, to humans as well.

From her past and what she knows today, Hui particularly likes to tell children that chickens are individuals with distinct characteristics. They deserve a natural life: scratching, clucking and running freely.

To dear friend Bob who helped make my Chicken Dream carried from Beijing, China come true in Nova Scotia, Canada

Running Wild with Bossy Boy

Not far from St. Margaret's Bay in Nova Scotia, Canada, there is a beautiful country yard spotted with many gardens and surrounded by evergreen woods.

Among several buildings, a small house looks quite different.

Besides a regular door and a window, it has a small entrance just above the ground. This entrance is opened and closed daily from outside by a rope passing over a pulley.

On one side, the little house has a protected coop deep-wired into the ground. No wild animals such as raccoons, foxes or falcons can dig under, bite through or fly into it.

A dead pine tree top, stretching several long bare branches, is installed and stands in the centre of the coop.

Inside the little house looks special, too. Fresh hay on the floor and in two rows of nests provides a sweet aroma.

Sun shines through a big window and sometimes light streaks shimmer in the air.

Two fine oil paintings hang on the walls. One has colorful flowers and the other is of a proud rooster standing tall. What a cozy little house it is!

Does anybody live here?

Yes, a flock of lucky chickens lives in this cozy house.

The house and the coop keep them comfortable, safe and warm especially during cold winters in Nova Scotia.

2

As a flock, they are social and do many things together.

When snow melts and spring shifts to summer, the big country yard outside the coop becomes their real paradise.

There, they run wild foraging tender greens, chasing flies, catching fast-jumping grasshoppers or scratching through piled-up old leaves to look for worms, bugs and pupa.

Once they are full from these daily feasts, they enjoy stretching out on the soft grass under the sun,

Crowding together on an old wooden garden bench,

Or roosting in the shade on the lower branches of the tall trees surrounding the yard.

Sometimes they sit in a spot with loose dirt and gradually dig out a body-sized hole. Things then become quite busy—feet scratching hard, dirt flying up and wings flapping fast to spread the loosened dirt through their feathers.

What are they doing? They are taking a dirt bath!

Can dirt make them clean? Yes!

After about thirty minutes, they stand up flapping and shaking off the dirt along with anything else unwanted. Next, they start to preen themselves with their beaks by pulling on and straightening out their feathers.

Having had a dirt bath, they feel fresh and clean.

When the sun is at its highest in the sky, they know it's time for a nap. Still they keep searching for one more "snack", while slowly walking in the direction to the coop.

Before sunset, no matter how joyfully they have played outside for the day, they always make their way home and roost together for the night in the cozy little house.

Although they do things together in a well-built order, called a pecking order, they are easily identified from one another by their remarkable characteristics and distinct personalities.

"Personalities?" Yes, chickens have personalities or specifically called "chicken-alities".

In other words, chickens are individuals and differ from one another. Some are brave and some timid; some are fighters and some peace keepers; some are determined and some hesitant; some are simple and some complicated.

They show basic emotions such as happiness, fear, anger and favorites or preferences in different ways.

Thus, every chicken living in the little house has earned a well-suited name.

• Bossy Boy •

In their pecking order, **Bossy Boy** is at the top of the flock. With his chest puffed-out and head held high, there is no mistaking his confidence, boldness and commitment to his flock.

His typical Plymouth Rock snowy-white feathers with a contrasting black-tip pattern, a red face and an upright comb make him the most distinctive bird in the flock.

No one can dispute his well-deserved name and no one dares challenge his top position.

In fact, Bossy Boy is not only a boss; he is a guard, provider and peace-keeper with many responsibilities on his mind.

In the beginning, when Bossy Boy was just a big white chick, he showed his natural talent and superb skills for looking after the others.

When the other chicks were busy taking dirt baths, Bossy Boy did not join them because somebody must stand guard. Who would be that somebody? No doubt, it's Bossy Boy!

Every morning, Bossy Boy is always the first one rushing out of the house.

He loudly flutters his wings, looks around and takes his measured steps to the centre of the coop.

There, for all to hear, comes his crowing of a "Cock-a-doodle-dooooo!" loud and clear to open a fresh day.

When the flock runs wild in the yard, Bossy Boy is always on duty. He keeps everybody in sight and clucks with a warning tone to alert of something suspicious, dangerous or threatening.

No matter how far Bossy Boy is from their house, he never drops his guard on it for one second as he knows the hens lay eggs there.

So don't let Bossy Boy sense somebody is heading towards the big door of the chicken house to pick up eggs from the nests.

Otherwise, he will ruffle the feathers on his neck and race at rooster lightning speed to the house.

He always arrives in time through the small entrance — the chicken door. Once face-to-face with the "burglar", Bossy Boy challenges by lowering one wing, tangoing around and then thundering in his throat.

"Goo, Goo, Gooo . . . Hey, I bet you won't dare take ONE MORE STEP!"

Whenever he finds food, he makes a special call, his food call "Koo-Goo, Koo-Goo, Koo-Koo-Goo." He repeatedly picks up and drops what he has found as if to say, "Come here! I found something tasty!" Bossy Boy seldom eats the tasty food, letting others enjoy first.

What a generous and selfless rooster Bossy Boy is!

In the evening, Bossy Boy waits in the coop for the others returning to the house. As the last one to enter the house for the night, he likes to see no one is missing and everything is secure.

All the chickens love Bossy Boy. They feel safe, satisfied and comfortable living with him.

12

• Brother Roosters •

Don't expect all roosters to be like Bossy Boy! Often, with some of the brothers, there are troubles for Bossy Boy to manage.

Thump, Thump, Thump, one after the other, here come **Long Legs** and **Crazy Legs**, two young Rhode Island Red roosters.

Long Legs is the tallest in the flock and Crazy Legs sometimes, for no apparent reason, suddenly crashes to his knees as if his legs are too weak . . . Or is it because he totally forgets to hold himself up?

These two roosters cannot stand to be near one another, so fights happen almost every day.

Look at their feathers! They have squared off, triggered at any time to jump into the air and kick at each other. It can be a long clash before they become too tired to keep on fighting.

Surprisingly, during their battles, Crazy Legs does not have any trouble with his knees. Thus, there are no advantages for Long Legs.

Their fights bother Bossy Boy. "I cannot stand unrest like this in the yard!"

"Hey, you two, STOP! How many times have I told you? No fighting!"

Bossy Boy must chase them apart, but he is never directly involved in their battles. Nobody doubts his authority to restore peace to the yard.

If Long Legs and Crazy Legs are two rowdy simple fighters, the next rooster is complicated and difficult to classify. His feet, like no others, are pink! Thus, he is named after the color: **Pink Feet**.

As a chick, Pink Feet was cute and seemed to be growing into a sweet hen.

When more feathers grew out, however, it became confusing.

"Are you a rooster or a hen, Pink Feet? Why do you like to follow the most beautiful hen in the yard and sit beside her? Why are you lurking around?"

One morning, Pink Feet disclosed the secret with a reedy and high-pitched "Cock-a-doodle-dooooo!"

Ha, Pink Feet, you are a rooster! Still, no one can determine exactly what is going on with this complicated brother.

Unlike Pink Feet, brother **Blackie** sounds muffled and deep, just like his body, thick and sturdy.

Everyone agrees Blackie is a handsome rooster and a typical "gentleman", but few notice his change from a little brown chick to a strong black-feathered red-face rooster.

He rarely pays attention to much of what happens around him. The big fights between Long Legs and Crazy Legs never bother him.

It doesn't matter to him if Pink Feet roosts nearby and behaves a little strangely. He seldom shows interest in the food calls from Bossy Boy.

It seems Blackie likes being alone and lives in his own world.

However, one day Blackie does something differently. On a summer afternoon, Blackie can barely walk and his red face looks pale. He is put into a big hay-filled box for examination and recovery. The box is kept in a shed far from the chicken house.

It seems impossible, but at sunset, when all the others are back home for the night, Blackie shows up. He is exhausted and hardly breathing. It's a mystery how he gets out of the box and drags himself all the way to the chicken house.

Could it be true that Blackie relates to the song, "There's No Place like Home"? Or in his heart, is there no place like the cozy little house?

Next morning, Blackie recovers and his face is as red as usual. He happily rejoins his brothers and sisters. Muffled and full bass-sounding crows from him soon echo in the yard.

There IS no place like home and family MATTERS to Blackie.

• Sister Hens •

Although sister hens do not cause any trouble for Bossy Boy as some roosters do, they surely show their unique characteristics and interesting chicken-alities.

Pretty Bird is the most beautiful hen in the flock. She is the same breed as Bossy Boy, a White Plymouth Rock. Her feathers are always clean, bright and well preened. She behaves like a proud princess.

She has no fear of being aggressive and pecking the roosters if they try to defy her superiority or become annoying. By nature shown early, Pretty Bird is the second in the pecking order behind Bossy Boy.

To other hens, she doesn't need to confront any of them because they know she is a fair sister. They understand each other.

This proud princess is also independent. Most times when the flock is out in the big yard, she is off hunting by herself.

She is particularly close to her human friends and considers them as part of "her family".

When they bend to clean the coop or to feed her and the others, Pretty Bird always finds reasons for jumping up on their shoulders and gently poking their hair with her beak. "Hey, your hair looks messy!"

Or she may curiously peck at their shirt buttons as if doing research. "What are these for, flat and round?" She loves pats on her back and head. Her feathers are smooth, soft and thick.

Lovely Pretty Bird, being the first one among all hens, laid her first egg when she was five months old. She has a well-tuned biological clock for laying eggs. Almost every morning at about ten o'clock, she quietly leaves the others to lay an egg in her favorite hay-filled nest.

One morning this routine is badly interrupted.

Around ten o'clock, instead of sitting in a nest, Pretty Bird paces anxiously outside of the house. She clucks differently and louder than usual. "Ger, Ger, Ger, GAR! Ger-GAR! Ger-GAR!" Smart Pretty Bird tries hard to communicate with her dear human friends in her own language.

She then jumps to one of the branches in the coop. "There is something I don't like in the house! Help! Help!"

"What's wrong in the house, Pretty? Is it catching fire or flooding?"

"NO! NO! WORSE THAN THAT! Ger-GAR! Ger-GAR-GAR!"

Her face turns bright red and she gasps for air as though she is choking. She clucks much louder.

What's really going on in the little house?

When the big door is opened wide, to everybody's surprise, Pink Feet, the complicated rooster, is sitting in Pretty's favorite nest and pretending nothing is wrong.

To Pretty Bird, the proud princess, what else could be more disturbing than finding her most important time of the day ruined by a rooster, especially by the sneaky rooster Pink Feet?

"Pink Feet, you really are a funny little rooster! What are YOU doing here? Never ever mess with a hen when she wants to lay an egg! Get out of here, you!"

Pink Feet is chased and has to abandon the nest. Is that the end to Pink Feet? Nooo! Listen!

When he hurries out the small door, his reedy high-pitched crowing is left dribbling in the air. "What's wrrrrong? I loooove Pretty Bird, tooooo!"

Ha! More is discovered about this complicated rooster, Pink Feet.

How did **Timid Hen**, a dark brown Rhode Island Red, get her name? It went back to her chick-hood.

In the early days, all baby chicks stayed in a house with their human friends. One day, a wooden spatula on a kitchen counter fell and hit the floor loudly. All the little chicks either jumped away or kept eating without paying much attention, except one who was scared

to death and sat frozen stiff on the floor. Timid, it was! No one else could deserve this name.

Soon, Timid grows into a beautiful but shy hen. She applies all her faint-hearted characteristics to her daily activities.

A gust of wind blowing the trees overhead or a black crow cawing from the sky is monstrous to her. She stops whatever she is doing, quietly finds the shortest path home and hides.

"Doesn't it scare Pretty Bird and other hens?" she wonders.

In winter, when snow covers the yard,

Timid Hen doesn't dare walk on it. She is afraid the snow will open up and swallow her.

She'd rather stay in one spot than run with others for food. Or she hops with fluttering wings from one rock or mound to another within a short distance. Poor Timid!

These are not the scariest things in her life. One day, something horrible indeed happens to Timid.

It is a lovely summer day. While the chickens roam in the yard, Oland, an energetic puppy dog, comes for a visit.

Oland finds the chickens and his eyes light up. "What do I see here? Chickens! I want to play!" He dashes joyfully across the big yard and pounces right in the middle of the chickens!

What chaos Oland makes! In a flurry, both hens and roosters cluck loudly as if they all have laid an egg. Flapping hard, they jump up and rush to the coop– all except one, Timid Hen, who goes missing.

The sun is sinking and night is falling, but still no Timid Hen. **"Where are you, Timid? Where are you?"**

It becomes dark and during the night, a blowing rainstorm sweeps over everything.

Next morning, it dawns fresh and clear. Searching far into the woods, a big matted pile of dark-brown feathers is spotted . . . **Oh, no!**

Moving closer to see, the pile is trembling! Yes, it is Timid Hen! She is alive but well-soaked, head buried under a wing and shivering hard — poor Timid.

How has she suffered through the downpour and survived the whole night alone? Which is more horrible to you, Timid? Is it little Oland or the storm, the shadows, the wild animals and the devilish sounds in the giant dark woods?

Poor Timid must have lost her direction for home when encountering Oland and fell in a heap in the woods.

It could only happen to this extremely timid girl, Timid Hen!

25

• New Chicks •

Four peeping chicks, two months old, are introduced into the flock. To them, joining the existing flock is not an easy adjustment.

Soon they learn their position . . . at the very bottom of the pecking order!

At first they hunt as a small group in the places where the older chickens seldom go, such as rocky slopes or far sides of the yard.

Later, they physically merge into the flock but still feel somewhat like outsiders.

Their arrival creates a great opportunity for rooster Long Legs. He temporarily directs his focus away from fighting Crazy Legs to looking after the new chicks. They welcome Long Legs because he makes them feel protected.

He loves to lead them around the yard to forage. If he thinks they have gone too deep into the woods, he calls them back . . . "Gook-Gook Goo."

Thanks to Long Legs, Bossy Boy's patrol becomes a little easier: wherever tall Long Legs is, all the new chicks are found.

Among the new chicks, one is quite small and in poor condition. It has a very bald back and tail. For these, **Poor Little** gets its name. The parts without feathers are of particular interest to the other three new chicks. They cannot help but peck at the "meat". Poor Little needs help and protection, but none of the ideas work.

First, the bald parts are treated with medicine. Every time Poor Little is held for treatment, it cries pitifully. Without question, it alarms Bossy Boy. "What's up over there? I must go check!" When Poor Little sees Bossy Boy's "ruffled neck feathers" coming at "rooster lightning speed", it cries even harder. That's it! No more treatment!

Instead, a specially-designed sleeveless sweater with braces and buttons is knitted. Resembling a short skirt, it fits Poor Little perfectly.

In spite of how perfectly it fits, within a few minutes, the little chick can magically escape from the well-tightened and well-braced sweater like a molting cicada casting off its shell.

Fortunately, Poor Little survives the trauma and he develops into a well-feathered handsome rooster!

His feathers have a reddish-golden color and his comb differs from the others. It is called rose comb and has rounded wrinkles. The reddish-golden feathers and the rose comb give Poor Little a very distinctive look!

No matter how handsome Poor Little becomes, he is never above himself because he still remembers his past — a poor chick with a bald back and tail.

The other three new chicks become hens.

Two of them are common in size, color and shape like twin sisters.

Every day, they go wing-in-wing to the woods and roost shoulder-by-shoulder on the same branch. It is difficult to tell them apart just like Tweedledee and Tweedledum in the book "Alice in Wonderland".

Here they are, **Tweedledee** and **Tweedledum**!

Sisters Dee and Dum deserve the names not only because of their looks, but because of their similar chicken-alities. Both are quiet, hesitant and sometimes overly cautious. They seldom make noise and no one has ever heard the usual clucks after they lay an egg.

It often appears sister Dee and sister Dum are looking at each other as if having a hard time to make the next decision.

Likely they have a fear of bothering anyone. Otherwise why do they tiptoe or edge away when the flock runs in the yard?

Hey, don't forget about **Yellow Bird**, one of the new hens with light yellowish-brown feathers.

Yellow Bird is a brave and tough girl!

Like Pretty Bird, she is close to humans but for different reasons.

She appreciates every comforting pat and every scrap of food to help her survive. She eats superfast because she has a strong belief that at the bottom of the pecking order, every peck should be a mouth-full and swallowed quickly.

After Yellow Bird starts laying eggs, none of the other hens can compete with her. She lays a brown egg every day and her eggs are the biggest of all the hens.

Unlike Pretty Bird, she is not picky about where to lay eggs and nothing can interrupt her routine. Contrary to Timid Hen, she has no fear of anything.

One evening, while searching for food late, she doesn't go home to roost but sleeps the night alone in the woods.

Is there any surprise the next morning? Yes, a big brown egg lies in the mossy woods, a beautiful daily gift from Yellow Bird—the tough, brave and adaptable girl.

• A Dedicated Mother •

Of all the hens in the flock, it is **Little Hen** — the smallest and the gentlest hen — that wants to be a mother.

On early summer days, Little Hen looks determined as day-after-day she sits on several eggs in a nest — she goes broody.

Don't even attempt being close to her nest! Otherwise this gentle hen opens her beak wide and shouts in defense, "Go, Go, Go away!"

Day and night, Little Hen patiently sits on the eggs. She sometimes gently turns them with her beak and rarely does she leave the nest to eat or drink.

Three weeks later, "Peep, Peep, Peep," comes from the nest.

Three cute hairy chicks, Little Do, Little Re and Little Mi, Do-Re-Mi, one after the other hatch into this world!

33

Without any break after the hatching, exhausted mother Little Hen starts to teach her babies. She picks up a piece of food but quickly drops it. She picks up another piece of food and drops it again. What is she doing? She is showing her babies what to eat and how to eat.

She always lets them stay around her, crawling on her back, hiding under her wings or peeking out from her chest.

She remains alert at all times. If she thinks something is dangerous, she calls, "Goo, Goo, Goo." Do, Re and Mi, on hearing Mom's call, quickly follow her to the house.

Nights do not belong to mother Little Hen either.

When other chickens are up on poles or wood benches to roost for the night, she sits on the hay-covered floor, halfway opening her wings and puffing her chest for Do, Re and Mi to sleep beneath.

She selflessly provides a warm, safe and comfortable place for her babies.

Quickly, Do, Re and Mi become too big to cover, but they still cry, "I want Mommy! I want Mommy!" She stretches her wings over them the best she can.

Isn't Little Hen a dedicated mother!

Soon summer passes. **Little Do** and **Little Re** become two good-looking young roosters.

Their feathers are snowy white with a black-tip pattern on their necks and tails, similar to Bossy Boy.

Their fights, however, are at an upgraded level from those between Long Legs and Crazy Legs.

Bossy Boy seems tired from stopping battles, but being a peace-keeper, he has no choice.

He must impose the ban on these two emerging fighters.

At the same time, sweet **Little Mi** grows into a lovely hen. Being brought up solely by chicken mother Little Hen, this little girl behaves a bit wild and is not close to humans.

A soft pat to her is not acceptable and she must peck it away. She is not interested in the scraps that Yellow Bird happily grabs by the mouth-full.

She never jumps onto any human's shoulder, pokes at their hair or studies shirt buttons as Pretty Bird does.

Is a gust of wind or a black crow coming? Little Mi doesn't care because mother Little Hen has always managed these for her.

Her chicken-ality tells everybody: "I am different!"

• Country Yard Symphonies •

These are the real stories of Bossy Boy, his brothers, his sisters and Do, Re, Mi, growing up from baby chicks to roosters or hens.

Every day, each shows the unique characteristics and interesting chicken-alities freely. Every day, "Symphonies" from them arise here and drift there into the woods surrounding the country yard.

Shhhhh . . . Listen!

"Gerrr, Gerrr, Gerrr, Gerrr . . ." It is **Little Hen,** with gentle clucks swirling in her throat, roaming and wondering where her babies might be though they are no longer babies. "Oh, here you are **Little Mi.** Don't jump . . . it's dangerous! **Little Do** and **Little Re,** where have you gone?"

"Ger, Ger, Ger, Ger-Gar." ". . . Ger, Ger-Gar." **Yellow Bird** and **Pretty Bird** proudly report to the whole world: "We laid eggs today."

"You go first," says sister **Dee**.

"No, no, no, after you," responds sister **Dum**.

"Should we go together?" . . . they ask each other.

"**Timid**, come over here!"

"Is Oland there?"

"No, Timid, there is no doggy Oland today!"

Pink Feet tries hard to bring his high pitched "cock-a-doodle-doo" to everybody's attention.

After the high pitched tune, here comes a deep muffled call from **Blackie**, the sturdy and typical "gentleman".

Flap, Flap, Flap, is there a peacock fanning its tail in the woods? No, no, it is **Poor Little.** He is loudly fluttering wings to show off his beautiful reddish-golden feathers.

Thump, Thump, Thump, **Long Legs** and **Crazy Legs** are still chasing each other at full speed!

"Hey you, Little Do, Little Re, you . . . you stay away from each other!" shouts **Bossy Boy.**

* * *

Seasons rotate, leaves turn colors and new feathers replace old ones. What stays the same is this flock of lucky chickens enjoying a natural chicken life, **Running Wild with Bossy Boy** in their beautiful country yard.